The Foliage in the Underworld

By the same author

Woodcuts.

Loose Federation (with Julian Croft)

Dawn Parade

Barbarians

Braindamage Festers and a Louisville Fordtruck Songbook

Robert Solay's Dreaming

In Twenty Years: Poems for Shelton Lea

The Way It Is: Selected Poems

Another Feast After Famine

Alive in Difficult Times

Look, He Said: Poems 1994

Strange Journey

Waiting for Rain: More Love Poems

Waiting for Rain: 10 Songs (Libretto for score by Rolf Gehlhaar)

Park

Poems 2001

History: Selected Poems 1978-2000

The Sweeping Plain

Another Fine Morning in Paradise

Apollo in George Street: The Life of David McKee Wright 2012.

The Poetic Eye: Occasional Writings 1982-2012

In the Real World (and other poems)

Many Such as She: Victorian Australian Women Poets of World War One.

The Foliage in the Underworld

Michael Sharkey

PUNCHER & WATTMANN

First published in 2019

Published by Puncher & Wattmann
PO Box 279
Waratah NSW 2298

http://www.puncherandwattmann.com
puncherandwattmann@bigpond.com

ISBN 9781925780604

NATIONAL
LIBRARY
OF AUSTRALIA

A catalogue record for this book is available from the National Library of Australia

Printed by Lightning Source International

Front cover photograph: Michael Sharkey, Lychakiv Cemetery, Lviv, Ukraine, 15 June 2013
Back cover photograph: Specialty Studio, Piccadilly Arcade, 200 Pitt Street, Sydney, 1949

Cover design by Miranda Douglas

To the memory of Muath Safi Yousef al-Kasasbeh,
murdered in Raqqa, January 2014,
and other sentient beings, victims of human cruelty

Contents

The Common Room

Poem with Aunts, Vase and River   11
First Eleven   13
The Year my Voice Broke   16
Here Lies   17
Pierre Ryckmans is Dead   18
The Consolation of Philosophy   19
Clinical Trials: 21
      Readers Digest   21
      The Root Canal Called Love   24
      Just Look at Yourself   27
In Bed With You   31
The Common Room   33
Going Nowhere Fast   37
Dead Man in a Pitt Street Jeweller's Doorway Anno 1966   40
Gert By Sea   42
The Lay of the Land: 44
      Customs Declaration   44
      The View from the Pornopticpon   45
      Could Anything be Wetter?   46
      Time and Motion   47
      To What End, Then?   48
Lviv   50

The Good Life And Others

Poem: That Looks Like Fun   55
The Cycle Path: A Walk in the Throwaway World   56
Aplomb   58
Field Study   59
Private Views   60
My Swedish Life   61
Tales Out of School: 63

He says, She says   63

A Gift for Teaching   64

Introduction to Composition 100   65

The Visiting Preacher Spoills the Good Oil on Acne at the Retreat   66

And So Goodnight   67

Defriend Me Here   68

The Pursuit of Happiness   70

The Good Life When It Happens   72

Grafton Bridge   74

Listening to the Prime Minister   77

John On Patmos   79

The Simplicity of It   80

The Stranger in the Crowd   82

City Circle   83

Impromptu   85

A Bird at Evening   86

My Parents Don't Exist   87

Returns of the Day   89

Nudge Nudge   90

My Life as a Cowboy   91

Wotif   92

Catullan Farewell   95

To Silence   96

Acknowledgements   97

The Common Room

Poem with Aunts, Vase and River

My mother and my father are in bed and it is Sunday.
This is Kogarah, and I cannot reach the handle.
I wonder why big people close the doors to read the paper.
My father's parents live across the hall.

Now we're in a house that disappears because of children.
Uncle Jack and mother's sister Edith come to visit. 'She says, "Jack, Jump",
and Jack jumps', my father says. They're more old-fashioned than my
parents.
I'm in bed with fever and a teddy. Abscess this time, after mumps.

That's my cousin Adrian on the verandah with no pants on.
When I ask my mother, she says he's a saucy fellow, and calls,
'Edith, just see what that boy of yours has got his hands on'.
My aunt Edith says, 'That little bugger'. He starts yelling,

for the flogging that my uncle Jack will serve him.
All these people who are dead now fill our lounge with their palaver.
This is years before Aquarius. It's Friday Catholic Fish night.
I am putting shellac records back inside their paper covers.

Father's mother says, 'Don't say Beef Oven say Bait Hoven'.
She says 'When I was a girl I heard the Navy bands play marches
when the Big White Fleet arrived. I wish that Mollie'd kept up playing
violin.
The ships were on the Point before they built the Harbour arch'.

My parents' parents all drew breath before the old Queen died.
A century unravels in my mind. What was it like then? Bullock drays and
carts.
They told me, 'Don't ask questions, play outside'.
They're living gargoyles shuffling memories like cards.

The great aunts are as old as I am now. Their heads are papery and white.
Their father's fathers had the knack of losing property and cash.
My mother's side are Cashmans, Egans, Moirs, Smiths and Wrights.
This one had cancer. That one drowned inside a well. Heart. Fatal crash.

Two ways you can go about a thing. One is correct, and one is Wright.
Two of the great uncles are alive. One went to France. I have his stamps.
The antique one insists that great aunt May give him his rights.
He calls them conjugals. My mother's look at me says, 'Do not ask'.

My great aunts' rooms are tinctures, talc, milk arrowroot and tea.
Aunts live for years. One kicks a dissolute son out.
Another spends her life in church and bedroom on her knees
entreating God to take the sod who keeps her poor. God doesn't care.

God's son is a sad sack hairy man who wears his heart outside his vest.
He watches from the glass's other side. He stares at me.
The devil's much more busy everywhere. I like him best.
He's very good at what he does. I'm smacked and told I'm talking blasphemy.

My mother's favourite aunt is ill, the one who lives alone.
She always did. My mother and I board a DC3. I sleep. She moans.
My mother says her aunt was disappointed years ago.
I am too young to know by heart what disappointment means.

My mother's aunt is dressed in tactile black. Her manners are immaculate.
Her row of standard poets frames her chair. The silverware she eats from bears
        a crest.
A khaki river flows beside her street. A paddle steamer on the bank's a wreck.
A crystal's sunbeam livens peacock feathers in a vase.

First Eleven

My father's arm inside a cow.
The tractor's wheels. The neighbour's plough.
My uncle's hat. Big silo rats.
My Bunny Plate. My tripe. My brains.
The half-ripe figs. My stomach pain.
My sick in bed. My mother's bread.
My first green pea. My cup of tea.
My box of blocks. The wind-up clock.

My measles. Mumps. My chicken pox.
My father's shotgun and the fox.
My ding dong bell. Cat's in the well.
Old English Rhymes. First writing book.
My mother's high heels from Mark Foy's.
The cowboy suit in Children's Toys.
My sailing boat. My rubber duck.
My nail in foot. My bad haircut.

My ugly boils. The castor oil.
My clockwork train. My Snakes and Ladders.
Uncle Bloo whip-cracked an adder.
The fruit in jars my mother cooked.
My *Little Engine That Could* book.
My *Playhour* comic. Billy Brock.
My Ovaltine. My funny dream.
My aunt's green stamps. The gypsy camp.

The doctor heating up a shot.
The hospital. The fever chart.
Pounds, shillings, pence. The barbed wire fence.
My metal Black Boy money box.
My great-aunt's pride. My first horse ride.
My flour and water pasted scraps.
Heroic British Empire chaps.
My *National Geographics* stacked.

The Royal Visit. Easter Show.
My sherbet packet. Liquorice stick.
My shop-bought pie. My Iced Vo-Vo.
My Cracker Night. My Jumping Jack.
My father's gas mask. Helmet. Tunic.
My small sister in the clinic.
My six-stitcher. My first duck.
The choko vine. The dunny truck.

My enemies. The policeman's son.
The Presbyterian School Gang.
My Catholics Catholics Ring the Bell.
Big Manuel can go to Hell.
My sticks and stones. My fight.
My speed. My cubby house. My wattle tree.
My circus pass. The clown on fire.
My father's cousin drives a Riley.

Stamps from Saxony and Hesse.
Who spilt Brylcreem on the dresser?
Peter Dawson. Roy Rene Mo.
My dog called Tim. The postman's fright.
My cousin's death. My free to roam.
My pencil case. My Globite bag.
My twelve times tables. Jack the lad.
My spelling bees. My trophy cards.

My abscessed ears. My months in bed.
My Ratty Badger Toad and Mole.
My Treasure Island. Ivanhoe.
My Captain Nemo. Chingachgook.
My Rina Ketty. Charles Trenet.
La Mer. La Ronde de L'amour.
My Tournent tournent beaux paysages.
Jussi Björling. Jack Teagarden.

My thick uniform. My cap.
My football boots. My running shorts.
The bindi-eyes. My naked feet.
My school war cry. My losing team.
My jokes. My teacher's 'Who said that?'
My long way home. My late for tea.
My choir practice. Schubert Lieder.
My cold lamb chop. Muddy knees.

My model plane. My game of cards.
My grandma's rowboat on the lake.
My Christmas. Thinnest slice of cake.
My verandah bed. My lie awake.
My singalong. Old vaudeville songs.
My leatherjacket. Whiting. Bream.
My gutting knife. My slippery hands.
My mullet's scales. I think I can.

My mother's roses. Dad's cigars.
My Bunsen burner. Dinky cars.
My First in English. First in Class.
My first and only first and last. My diving mask.
The ocean bed. *Around the World in Eighty Days*.
Another younger sister's birth.
Three grandparents gone to earth.
My dead. My genes in photographs.

The Year My Voice Broke

Back in the days when news was sometimes focused
on what really seemed important, like the ice-cream
family block that came in a waxed box
on the table, and a scoop of plain vanilla
in a glass of Coca-Cola was a class act
in a milk bar called the IXL or Empire
and the sliced meat on our sandwiches was devon,
some said fritz, and we knew the world
that we inhabited was free, unlike the others',
and the white guy in the sky was backing
our side, and our beaches were the finest
and our sheep the world's most sheepish
and our Stamina school uniforms ensured
that we were equal to each other
while Hungarians and Russians were at war
in a Melbourne swimming pool, and the thought
of sex was frightening, plummy accents
on the radio announced that, unbelievably,
a Commie dog was flying round the world.

Here Lies

My brother's dog is dead and I can't do a thing about it.
Dog days now for dog, and brother
dogged by reminiscence, curtailed walkies. Other
dogs are barking, but his caravan's moved on.

Dog my brother called dog for all seasons,
dog for giving dog a good name.
Dog now image, silent movie? No-
dog night, now cold as dog's nose.

Dog for sitting in a tin boat while my brother poached blue swimmers.
Dog for splashing out, a Pudel.
Dog for giving tongue. A goner.
Dog embarked for Cytherea.

Dog for sniffing dog-piss in the park and on the pavement.
Dog turned abstract, disincarnate,
dog on leash tugged tight by death. No-
doggone zen of no-dog barking.

Dog my bones, can't whistle dog up,
dog meat, now, old dog-eared tale.
Dog it was that died, and dog
still walks my brother's mind, its spelling back to front, wo-ow.

Pierre Ryckmans is Dead

Friday's paper in the morning train holds little else that's worth recalling.
Fellow passengers sit silent or talk carelessly aloud on mobile phones
As if asserting they are living, it's important, and it is.
A gentleman brings out the good in people.
He does not bring out the bad. The vulgar do the opposite.

Two teenage girls critique their part-time jobs and full-time friends.
They say 'That sucks'. The theme of this year's Halloween is Hos
and Pimps. One girl assures her friend she'll pluck her eyebrows,
just enough to have a line. 'Boys who have blue eyes are hot',
says the other. 'I can't wait to get at the Kahlua',

When our betters cultivate civility,
the people are led easily, as Simon Leys observes
in his translation of the *Analects*.
I meditate on this while this train passes kangaroos en route to the city.
Just how tractable am I? Perhaps I'm not an ideal subject.

Youth creates itself by youth. They chatter on.
Experimenting with their tone of voice. They sound like movies.
What could these young people think of Ryckmans? And why should they?
Who believes that everything's transmitted to the young?
Age is not a mirror of the thing the young imagine they'll become.

If they have faults, they will discard them
or enjoy observing those of other people.
It's the fate of those who grow old to be judged
by others who are not their equals.
All that can be said is some will merit better obits.

The Consolation of Philosophy

My former girlfriend, of whom I have many,
shacked up with that jock from Double Bay.
Cocaine and a Boxster put her in the family way.
Johann Bernhard Bach wrote suites in several keys.

The Deuce, it's said, is with us everywhere.
The country's leader speaks to us in tweets.
Antigonus was eaten by a bear.
The sky is always grey above Trier.

The mussels open in the sizzling pan
like tabernacle doors and spit at God.
Some people should be banned from using phones.
Most perfumes have disgusting undertones.

Life's a diatonic run of notes.
The custom of the country's battering wives
and screwing children got by former wives.
My natal state is covered in black smoke.

A killer's eating ice cream in the Mall.
When mud dries out it is not longer mud.
The factory owner's daughter cops a feel.
We still recall the dead as full of blood.

I loved morphine till it gave up on me.
We were the only couple in the room.
Too busy with the world spirit to know,
when Debbie left I didn't see her go.

We called the police who didn't give two fucks.
You could have cut the cackle with a knife.
If this is what they call first class, it sucks.
I need to raise a fighting fund for life.

My ties from Georges de Paris are surreal.
What Jim calls having fun is no big deal.
Freak weather brought out thousands to the beach.
Each day since I've grown old, I eat a peach.

The house my mother lived in disappeared.
I said there was a cow beside my bed.
Too bad we didn't save the evidence.
The tree still hangs in sky inside the pond.

A drear deft wind went sifting through Navarre.
Guess who'll be going walkies in an hour.
I had a spotted Tim whose name was dog.
Some things could be worse than a French pissoir.

I'm not so taken with subjunctive mood.
My friend from Pécs was knocked out by a stroke.
I never thought to see so many cark.
We stayed in bed for days and read our skin.

The farms up here are full of rusting steel.
The kitchen's full of kipple and decay.
You say you're off to Pyonyang just for kicks.
We never spoke like this when we first met.

The lobster from the coral orchard dies
in agony en route to make a snack.
Meanwhile kabuki we call life goes on.
St Anthony preached happily to fish.

Death's a dog that runs toward me grinning,
barking, *In your end is my beginning.*
I wouldn't want to live my life again.
The four orchestral suites are what remain.

Clinical Trials

1. READERS DIGEST

In the waiting room I feel like someone with a gong,
Olympian among the walking wounded huddled there.
Their history's written in their busted mugs.
I feel like Rilian in *The Silver Chair*.

I've walked in on *The End of the Affair*.
They're reading dated *Who* and *Marie Claire*.
That one's about to die. A *New Idea*.
What movie am I in? *Hangover Square*?

Panadol makes red blood cells grow small
and pale and cark. I read about it in *New Scientist*.
Lighting up a smoke, my last quack told me, 'Sod it all,
just up your red wine intake and get pissed—

orange juice in moderation's fine
but takes its toll on kidneys, teeth and gums, and heart and eyes.
Besides, you'll find Sildenafil—Viagra, vulgarly—
works strangely with a grapefruit's extra C'.

For kicks I've read the labels on the packs
while waiting at the cut-price pharmacy.
Whatever blocks a pain has side effects
from going mad to cashing in the chips.

At night I read in bed till letters blur,
and I am left with solitude and blank.
Plutarch was Charlotte Corday's Goodread,
One side effect was that her body shrank.

The writing on an ancient metal tube
in MR James's ghost tale sent its finder round the twist.
I wake each day in darkness, open blinds
and watch the spooky trees in ebbing mist.

Reading, I inhabit every time and every place,
a cat for whom all backyards are as one.
Most narratives are boring. Mine is not.
I've read while someone next to me was shot.

I don't like making fun of other folk
especially when their lives read like a joke
tucked in a Christmas cracker. Mine, to others
makes them think with pity of my mother's.

At length, my mother croaked. She went aloft,
or so my sisters said, to join the Throng
Invisible and sing. They must be soft.
She said all hymns were naff and priests were nongs.

When citizens lament a leader's death
until the next one gives them better cause
to weep, I recollect what Tolstoy said
concerning convicts voting for the laws.

History often stutters, sometimes rants
and always ballses up the plot. At first,
you think it's *Wacko; Here we Go*—
and next time it's the *Rocky Horror Show*.

From time to time good nations run amok
and students beat professors to a pulp.
I've been in cities where canals ran red
and parents fled from children chanting crap.

When young, I read pulp fiction in between
Sic fatur lacrimans, you know the rest.
I partied like the party out of town
I'd read about in the *Decameron*.

The waiting room receptionist ignores
the walking dead among whom I've been cast.
My neighbour reads *Dirt Action*, I, *Fly Life*,
and check out girls on covers of *Get Lost*.

2. THE ROOT CANAL CALLED LOVE

If only love and wurst could rhyme as easily as this,
Would life be bliss?
Who has the time?
The world turns brown, the woods decay
And teeth grow loose as lovers' vows.
No man is a hero to his dentist,
And my last had disconcerting taste in art.

I might have pardoned much
But manga dogs and happy fish?
They creeped me out.
I didn't like the way he shook and twitched.
Perhaps he'd spent too much time on procaine.
He said 'This sure will hurt you more than me'.
I thought he was a weird son of a bitch.

The needle goes in, and I think
If life were longer, I could see myself as others.
But why bother? Easier to fill in time that's shorter,
Have a daughter who's a tartar,
See how simple it could be to grow
Much younger than I am,
And far more fun than being dead.

Serious intellectual life is missing
From this poem. Until now.
What's the bet Chris Brennan felt the same
Recalling Virgil while a harlot chewed his pencil
In a bedsit in a lane,
And hoods with razors and bad breath
Cut pretty figures while a Beale piano played.

The bigamist who ran the Black Cat café sat
And picked his teeth out back.
Was that thing that Phil and I saw Vernon,
Dead as mutton on the steps or merely zonked?
Who gives a rat's?
Beavers' teeth keep growing, just like mice,
It's why they gnaw.

In junior high school, colleagues dreamt of sex
And chewed their pencils and defaced their physics texts,
And handed filthy pictures under desks.
The classroom smelt of wet dreams.
Some chaps groaned.
I hear a lot of them are feeding worms.
Before the revolution life was sweet.

Nature studies showed me hymenoptera have teeth
That suck and chew,
But not how caterpillars understand the work they do.
Is there a Voltaire in their ranks?
Do sawflies think of sex while laying eggs?
I think of this each morning on the train
While I watch kangaroos at graze.

Kangaroos and sharks and manatees
Regrow their teeth.
Their diet is a riot. So is mine.
I snack on olives and pistachios.
My dental surgeon tells me tiny fragments lurk in bowels
And cause cancer. What of that?
I order a martini extra dry and write a line.

It all comes back. I floss my fangs.
I'm not a forest ranger, but there isn't much
About receding gums that I don't know.
The nurse's shadow falls across the window.
I'm inventing a new present to myself.
I've had a gutful of the past.
It doesn't last.

Or if it does, it seems to me I've rediscovered zero,
Travelled in the fifth dimension,
Met a pretty polytope and chewed the fat
And joined a travelling penteract.
Whatever they've been drinking in that cell,
Please spare me that, a molar mass.
A man's a mat in love. Take that.

3. JUST LOOK AT YOURSELF

The codger with the rheumy eyes tries looking at his hand,
and gives up, staring into space.
His funeral.
The oculist's receptionist calls, 'Next'.
A sign out front says 'Like us on Facebook'.
The buzzword of the business is Eye Care.
The Age of Nice is with us everywhere.

Ms Tan, my ophthalmologist, declares,
'The image on the screen's your eye's back wall.
You see the red lines on the orange orb?'
'You're sure that's not the planet Mars', I ask,
'There's water down there, alien life perhaps'. She beams me up:
'Are your eyes sometimes gritty, like with dust?
That indicates your blood pressure is up'.

I like the way she dodges round the catachrestic 'we',
unlike the people in the shop next door
with their 'Good morning, sir, and what would we be looking for?'
The eye is an extension of the brain,
and made up of three chambers—like the ear,
frogs' hearts, and Synod of the C of E –
which all work when each section does its part.

Virgil says *Sunt rerum lacrimae* –
that there are tears for things, and mortal things affect the mind.
Ms Tan says tears flow down the fronts of eyes
to drain in puncta and through ducts,
which, put succinctly means that when you've got
hysterics from your laughing
or convulsions from your grief, you're full of snot.

Cats' physiology is otherwise.
Their corneas don't require lubricating all the time.
Mehitabel and Felix and Sylvester
simply close their eyes or stare.
And if they wink,
they don't need glasses or a shrink.
They've got cat herpes. Call the vet.

Grief occurs like sudden squalls of rain
or abscessed ears' incessant pain. Fondling his cane,
my high school mathematics teacher told me, 'Look at you'.
Impossible, I told him: even in a mirror
I do not appear the same.
'So then we see each other in the Cubist light again' – his very words.
And after flogging me, he went on blithely drawing surds.

My friend who's going blind does not enjoy
the monthly needle in the eye. You get the picture.
Nor would I. He and others,
e.g., Milton, Borges, Joyce and Leggott,
have recalled the shapes and colours of the world.
But how could Homer illustrate the tincture of the sea,
the legend on Achilles's shield, what banners Strife unfurled?

And what do cyborgs know of fate,
or why a non-transhuman, such as I, drinks single malt?
What do they see and know of love?
Robots comprehend fatigue and stress and creep, I know.
It's in their programs where what we might label thought is shaped,
but do they know why people (I speak loosely of my species)
aren't, by and large, enamoured of disfigurement and rape?

At Sydney University, the gargoyles in the Quad
are said to portray scholars who worked there.
I've met some living lookalikes on Dublin's Grattan Bridge
and in the mirror shaving with a hand opposed to mine.
My uncle used to say come in and give the dog a fright.
It's always dark inside a poem.
'Now read out the smallest line', the elder partner says.

Ms Tan goes to the lab to check the script.
I put on my old glasses and peruse a magazine.
What's great about Palladio's palazzi is
their fronts, which though appearing false, are not.
Each building is a symphony in stone,
its symmetry unlike my poorer sight's.
I realise a weak pun in that line.

A Blind Man parks outside the convent gate.
The Abbess looks him up and down and asks,
'So you're the Blind Man?'—'Yes', he says, 'I am'.
I think I'll leave the punch line out this time.
Another blind man walks into a bar, a stool, a table....
The history of Byzantium's a maculated fable
pocked with tyrants blinding one or both eyes of their rivals.

Among the pleasures of the blind: graffiti:
they're spared that. Among the ones they'll never know:
a tree hangs upside down against the blue sky in a pond,
and Gemma the retriever with her mistress
every morning in the park, when traffic slows
and drivers take note of the loveliness of both.
And one is blind.

Perhaps I'll look fantastic in new specs,
by Rodenstock, DG or Hugo Boss—
precision fashion billboard on my face,
but every face presents a parody
of something that I once imagined me.
I ask instead to see the knock-offs shelf
and settle for a satire on myself.

In Bed with You

To W.

I used to have a lot of stuff
And now I want to ditch it.
I used to be a fussy cook,
And now I keep it simple.
Once I was apart from you,
But now I see you, face to face
What use are poems to me?

Nothing is impossible.
Your Sar-i-Sang lake-coloured eyes in LA
Put the Homeland in a spin.
The Mother of Republics
Said No Way when you walked in.
Your duffle coat and Handel score declared
They couldn't win.

In Ukraine we drank fresh young cabernet and ate grilled trout.
The Polish radar scanned Carpathian sky.
What did they think was coming through the rye?
A blink and modern history's trompe-l'oeil.
Your father's father's horses are long dead,
The soil around his village rich in blood.
White armies paid in bullets for their bread.

Democracies trip over time again.
In tyrannies, the people dream of wealth.
Spring's stubble grows across the country's face.
Developers see earth as unmade bed.
The day that we left Aachen in a train
The tops of trees were visible in flood.
We sipped a Winzersekt and watched the rain.

Brutus kissed the earth and founded Rome.
Six kookaburras call our garden home.
Rosellas storm the fruit tree out the back.
Each wing-flash quicker than a word misheard.
I feed the birds. You feed the birds.
They plunder what they lack.
The earth below is rotting apple wrack.

In flashback, where were we? Another day:
The wattlebird—a doting parent, that.
Let's stay another hour, so we stay—
Let's deconstruct the end of time, you say
The sun is in our sonnet, where we lie
And hear the town hall bell's inane low tone
count off its only purpose and our own.

That beauty is a weapon of disturbance is a fact.
Shrines to other creeds attract despair.
Some people do not act
from any sense that life is holy. They'll get theirs.
Beauty such as yours unsettles me.
Did I remark that your eye lashes me?
The life I knew would never be the same.

Why should nights have disappointing endings?
I, le Chevalier au Lion, say
that you are la Princesse de Lointaine.
I say that you vacationed from a dream.
When I consider how my time is spent,
the end of time has come and gone again,
and this chanson was heard in Aquitaine.

The Common Room

The foliage in the underworld is bleak.
It could be here. Developers have had enough of trees
and coral reefs. Eventually we'll put an end to these.
Ulysses and Aeneas down below converse in Greek.
Dante speaks good Florentine to all the spooks he meets.
Rimbaud's fiend eschews the Langue d'Oc.
Milton's snake and Eve are English speakers. So is God.

Les Murray (not the journalist) opined
a Common Room is where good talk is found.
The talk was mower blades when I looked in,
and not a word of Marvell, Clare or Frost.
Philip Larkin's Victa turned a hedgehog's flesh to grass
and grass to lawn. His elegy declared the act unkind.
Grass is punk to unobservant minds.

My mother used a formal English when she spoke to me,
which I gave back to her. What does this mean?
I could be her experiment in memory. Was it so?
Perhaps she outsourced hers. Who am I then?
If you lend books or money to your friends,
they'll turn amnesiac, she said. Skew-whiff, I write,
downloading poems from my head at night.

The work is like unscrambling omelette.
The world is apnoea and snap-awake.
Things are far more urgent than the right espresso blend.
It's me they're dropping bombs and rockets on
if I'm persuaded by each instant's news.
And it's no go morphine or Nembutal,
and no more passeggiata in the Mall.

Are people really happy on Nauru? Hands up who cares.
I nearly went to teach in high school there.
What use is knowing Milton and Rimbaud
when language has been stripped of all it holds?
The refugees we send there harm themselves.
It stops them harming anybody else.
What tense and mood's appropriate to those?

Thou shalt not speak in Turkish on the day
we celebrate as Anzac. Hip, hooray.
Another spiffing loss. Some win, some lose.
Nothing in the Dreyfus case was new.
It's said the Chinese are Jakarta's Jews.
There's always someone further down the line.
East Timor's off the map. I think your selfie's looking fine.

I'm lucky to be living in these times.
There's nothing but corruption in the east.
I can't believe a flood-prone patch of dirt
costs so much as our agent says it's worth.
'¡Viva la Muerte!' 'Get in Now!' 'Vogue la galère!'
We call a lie the truth and truth a lie.
And which is which you don't know. Nor do I.

I've met some people suave as you or me
in prisons where I tutored poetry.
I walked inside through several sets of gates
past warders who said, 'Let's hear you recite
"The boy stood on the burning deck" to crims'.
The warders spoke a whining dialect
that made me want to break their fucking necks.

I met a man who cut his dad in half
Because, he said, his father was a cunt.
He used a classic Henry Disston saw,
the choice of chippies who prefer the best.
His fellow inmates heard him out and laughed.
He mimicked how he held the bugger down
and took the head off first and then the rest.

I listened while he smoked a cigarette.
He said, 'Mum told me, "Keep your elbows in
while eating. Don't take up another's space"'.
'Good notion', I said, 'Keep on doing that,
and skip the soppy sentiments in verse'.
I said, 'Petrarchan sonnets mostly suck'.
'That's true', he said. 'I'd really like a fuck'.

The women's wing was sweetness and romance
if getting into some teenager's pants
is what the world calls love.
A florist told me, 'This is my new squeeze'.
When she got out, she said, she'd shoot the man
who'd failed to kill her rival down the street.
'Why spell it out in flowers, when a bullet's quick and neat?'

'For verse to your new love, Neoplatonic lyric's best,
and so's the post-Apocalyptic stanza. This is one.
Try writing them', I told her. 'Have some fun'.
She wrote 'Are you my true north, or my south?
I'd like to go to bed. I like your mouth'.
She said, 'I'm here until the dog-food years.
We'll live in parks. Read poems. I'm all ears'.

I liked her style. If irony's humanity's call-sign,
what's tragic? When my friend the poet died,
his daughters gathered in a church to boast,
'I am Cordelia, and I loved him most',
though one declared, 'I hated him, the swine'.
So much for piety and filial love.
It's hip to give benevolence the shove.

We're Hobbesian. Who doesn't have the strength
to bear the grief and suffering we see?
I count non-humans in our polity.
The bloody thing that's served up drenched with fat
that makes you think they've cooked the family cat
is this week's featured recipe.
Delicious. Don't hold back.

I celebrate the frog that knows to croak
is all a frog knows, in the pot when heat is on.
I've known a man grown frantic with the cries
of a koala dying from a tumour on its face.
He took the largest spanner from his truck
and beat the plaintive animal to death.
Could you or I do that? Don't hold your breath.

Going Nowhere Fast

The airport is my caravanserai,
a souk where I repose and offer thanks.
Poorer mortals chivvy whippersnappers
through the food hall's rationed bliss.
I put my trust in lounges where steel cutlery is used.
Sleek goddesses and gods take stock of Hermès and Tissot.
Please keep the tip. I shall not want.

It never was a doddle being me,
whatever that is. I have tried in several countries,
more than most will ever see.
Ascetics in their caves may travel free.
My self is in the locker when I board.
I see my fellow travellers are dressed to cut a dash.
I think we'll all look gorgeous if we crash.

I dine on tramezzino with a steely young Chablis.
I am my own imaginary, pushing borders back.
My body is a temple
and delights in Jura scotch.
My bible's the *Economist*. The latest is the best.
It guides me through the ravaged earth from leaders to obits.
I'll let you know where I am when I'm there.

I leave the largest island in the world,
its concrete paddocks by the sea.
The cocktails have arrived please make that two.
Each novel sight's a holiday I take from being me.
Squitch Fen is not the place I want to be.
John Bunyan wrote an alphabet of sighs and groans from hell.
I read *Supplément au Voyage de Bougaineville*. Farewell.

The runway is my Heimat

and my self is in the cloud.

My armchair is at rest between the troposphere and beach.

I cross brown deltas.

I'm inventing nation states.

Their borders are unclear as rivers changing names and shapes.

To starboard Finland's somewhere under scud.

To port is Leningrad or what its people call it now.

My nearest neighbour's semi-upright in 4B.

Her hair's a flock of frisking goats on Gilead.

She tells me she's in steel.

I tell her I'm in writing it's too late, I won't die young.

With every eyeblink, I'm in love with all things beautiful and bright.

I snooze and miss the no-time what-zone-is-it sambal snack.

Ice and snow's beneath me.

If I bailed out I would die.

The autopilot has the world I live in in its hands.

One of ours went missing some time back, but I should care.

The manual declares there is no joystick in this plane.

Degrees of criticality are easy when you know

the light turns amber first then red like Basel traffic lights.

The child of passion in row sixteen's

bringing down the house

except for Byrd's *laudate pueri* through my Bose headphones.

I'm easy in my slacks by Kathmandu and Swedish shirt.

I do the old soft Sioux and take my shoes off in the air.

On earth the crumpled fabric of a jacket labelled Boss

discreetly states the bearer can be found home anywhere.

When I lay me down to sleep
no myocardian infarct shall I fear.
I'm busy writing news that will stay news.
My writing is 2B and not 2B.
No desolation of abomination's near me in the stratosphere.
My notebook and my Lamy pen will surely comfort me.
The photo in my passport never was the me you see.

The German tourist falls down on her way back from the john.
Nobody told us theatre was included in the flight.
The cabin crew have bit parts with the doctor, whose vacation has begun.
The audience response is mixed. A number sympathise.
Some turn zen mind-murderers in silence. Some complain,
but surely gin and it will be with them for all their days,
for they have shot the breeze and they are high.

I've done with faux democracy.
I have seen that good and evil can exist in human hearts,
and self and nation's made from what one chooses to ignore.
To name and hold a misdeed is to see life fall apart.
Aloft, I know that death does not exist, and day is night,
and time is not a lump sum to invest. My time is life.
Dawn finds me rosy-fingered out of sight.

Dead Man In A Pitt Street Jeweller's Doorway, Anno 1966

The privacy we seek, you got in spades.
Pedestrians step over you
To see the rings and watches on display.
Some show annoyance, some disgust
At what you've done. I doubt you meant to end this way.
What were your last thoughts?
What was left for you to say?

I never heard your voice. I guess
It served you well enough in better times.
What other voices had you heard
Outside your head? The howl of crowds,
Or spoken bricolage of thought
Of partners in some skill or trade,
A family's repertoire of sighs?

I doubt I would have said a word
To what you were alive.
I talk aloud. Talk to myself?
The mystery of my craft. And yours?
Your face and hands are tanned.
Your arms that show from jacket sleeves
More pale. Were you a dandy?

Like the words in books that stay unread,
It's always like this, is it not,
When no one spoken to replies?
Your pockets are turned inside out.
The picture of your life.
Some wayfarer before I came
Made off with any profit.

Time has ceased.
What was your country? Was it mine?
You have no nation.
You are nothing that you were.
Pedestrians step nicely
Over you and round us both:
A gentle *ballet domestique*.

I almost missed you, unknown man.
Who will have eyes to miss you now?
Will anyone care where you're bound?
This doorway: good. The Janus touch.
You demonstrate what life is worth.
Including mine, my unknown friend.
Fare well.

Gert by Sea

Maui hauled a fish out of the sea.
Australia's Prime Minister was taken by Chinese.
Auckland's weekend sailors tried to stop a submarine.
I know it's true. I saw it. I was there.
Flotillas in our Dreaming left from Wellington and Perth
With people keen to lend a hand to fertilise the earth
In Turkey and in France. Give us a call.

We'd do it anytime. You all come back again, you hear.
On New Year's Eve in '69 I saw the sixties end.
The planes I flew in seemed much faster then.
A steward is a waiter in the sky.
Mine's a brandy, if you catch his eye.
Bombs were falling out like windblown seeds
To wipe out what were called the lesser breeds.

Who couldn't love the sixties who was there?
Wheat and wool kept Russians fed and snug.
The Rolling Stones were living in Kings Cross.
My girlfriend stole their liquor. Please return
To upright. We're commencing our descent.
To starboard see the Opera House and Bridge.
Dad bought Mum a Kelvinator fridge.

Read the *Sun*. Vacation in Fiji.
Kupe's fleet's approaching from the east.
Or is it west? Developers will be next, wait and see.
It's dog eat dog or *kuri*, who eat whom.
Now Mister Baxter's up the creek. He's found Jerusalem.
Parents, lock your daughters up from him,
And from his unseen friend that you will never meet. Amen.

The taniwha is turning in the tide.
Was that a bunyip you were with last night?
A ferry sinks. The Premier puts his cocoa to one side.
Morphine was amusing for a while.
You ever wonder why they call it dope?
The Pretty Things were banished after playing just one show.
The Premier puts his cardie on again and goes to sleep.

One side of the mainland looks to Dili,
And the Queen's son is a twit. He talks to trees.
Princess Anne is lovely and she stays at Cammeray.
The *Telegraph* reports on what she ate and wore today.
The Labor Party's ruled by Castro and the Viet Cong.
A man is hanged in Melbourne Gaol,
And their turn won't be long.

Vincent Eri's crocodile is waking from a kip.
There is an awful lot of coffee grown in PNG.
The Chinese own the main street.
The Koreans own the rest.
Rough sleepers fill the doorways of the Islands of the Blest.
We don't speak Eora here. Our Maori's not the best.
Is that Sherpa Tensing with Sir Bill on Everest?

Speak, Memory, Tok pisin. Dada went to fight the Hun
When pig iron turned to Zeroes in the Empire of the Sun.
Here's Gert out on the water on her boss's cruising yacht.
And here she's in her cossie at Balmoral looking hot.
In this snap of Darwin, she's relaxing at the club.
She's in the surf at Cottesloe
And raffled in the Bunch each evening, half a quid a go.

A dotted line around her neck is labelled Tear Off Here,
And Please Return to Sender's tattooed on her derrière.
She played in 'Nam, Afghanistan. She poses in khaki.
She's on the old Damascus Road she's visited before.
King Cnut in cross dress turning back the human tides,
Her halo is a rising sun of gleaming bayonets,
Her gifts a gutted isle, the killing fields, and suicide.

The Lay of The Land

'Really I'm just
a piece of meat'
'Meat', *Pieces of Intelligence:*
The Existential Poetry of Donald Rumsfeld,
ed. Hart Seely, New York: Free Press, 2003, p. 100

1. Customs declaration

Travellers in Porn report
        the landscape of the country
                is ignored by its inhabitants
                        who concentrate on work they have in hand.

These punters take no joy in what is round them.
        Coastal strip or mountain range
                or chic apartment, house and garden
                        are mere backdrop to their acts.
                                It is as if they are born blind.

Tourists to that country bring home narratives of customs
        that the rich and poor embrace, of rites
                that recreate the acts of gods, who knowing time was up,
                        in their panic took what pleasure they could snatch
                                from man or beast.

For all the energy the celebrants
        invest in sacred dramas of this sort,
                there is no sign their gods have heard them.
                        They are stuck with zero growth.

2. The view from the pornopticon

Endlessly they carry out the rituals
        that could be abstract expression,
            where the world is gestured at, refined to sport,
           to calisthenics and gymnastics,
             to Olympiads of sex.

Their routine's punishing
        as if they're sentenced prisoners
            determined to inflict their pain on others.
             Faces grimace.

We're the objects of their gaze,
        and what they do appears from angles
            no one in the scene can see.
             The Cubist touch.

3. Could anything be wetter?

They get right down to the bone,
              lap up each other,
                          and when they give up,
                                      licked, they kiss.

One is old enough to be the parent
              of the other: mother naked,
                          like the dialogue,
                                      reduced to bare essentials—

she with the grin of the cat-that-got-the-cream,
              and he with his wood-and-it-be-lovely
                          smirk.

Spielberg, eat your heart out,
              she says, while the one who's never
                          shown full frontal
                                      calls the shots,
                                                  but lets the fingers do the talking.

Germans call this Funktionslust:
              the pleasure one derives from doing
                          what one does so well.

4. Time & motion

Twelve hours on the set becomes the quarter of an hour
                   where it seems what they do best
                       will never end.
                             How do they stand the repetition?
                                 Why do those who watch all day?

No point asking which of them
                   has more fun than the other
                       in this hologram.
                             The actors, like the viewers,
                               have forgotten how to laugh.

Instead, eye-contact is the sales pitch.
                   Champ, the main event is you.
                       You're in there with the O-my-godding
                         puppets on a string,
                             in an apartment that we can't believe they live in
                                 where the sound's a metronome.

5. To what end, then?

At times, they grit their teeth so tight
        they cannot speak. At others,
                when their mouths are full, they can't.

They want it harder, want it longer,
        till, impossible, her howling him to stop,
            as if he could, as if she could.
                They soldier on, work-ethic's slaves.

How does it occur we'd have
        these people in our homes?
            Our proxy world—

the thought that one or both could die.
        Quel frisson: AIDS or suicide, or boredom.
            Gazers wedded to the postures,
                the appearance of assent,
                    the thought that we could do that too?

Why are the old and the ugly
        in such roles the meat for farce?
            The thought that power
                is the province of the young?
                Who holds the camera?

If this is an art a five-year-old can do,
        we're living in the province
            of the damned—
                the faces, bodies we can't get out from our minds.

And what they're doing—
        hand around a throat to choke a cry:
            apotheosis of this art?

When nothing is dysfunctional,
        and everyone's our meat,
                what's all the fuss?

6. Ancient snatches and lays

At Herculaneum, Pompeii, they were at it
        on the walls and floors
                of rooms where people met and spoke and ate,

and they are at it, at Ajanta, Khajuraho,
        after centuries,
                a drama that would make a mortal ache.

Lviv

I, too have been another person
in the coffee shops at dawn in other cities,
in the calm before the trams skirl round the corner of the square
where I am faced again with poverty of language I possess
and lack of time.

When sky turns halftone,
headscarfed women in blue uniforms sweep cobbled lanes and alleys
with rush brooms behind the rubber-tyred waste trucks,
so dew-washed faces of the buildings
and the watered facets shine.

The earthy perfume of the coffee,
scooped from sacks beside the roaster that turns berries darker still,
the labels, Cuba, Guatemala, Nicaragua, Colombia,
Jamaica, mapping people of the world I'll never meet:
their lives are private as my own, their thought as intimate,

and they remain anonymous as I, but we exist,
to bear each kiss or fear we've had or pain we gave,
till faces crumble, and our poetry grows bodiless
and eulogies are stale.
We find each other interesting, intricate.

My thoughts run on this way.
And then from brick and stone the click-click echo of tall heels –
how can these women on their way to sit in offices or stand
all day in stores the tourists haunt
proceed so steadfast and contained?
They cross themselves, like businessmen and students
passing by the pilgrim church; some bow, or nod or genuflect,
while others go without a glance, as if to pause
is to declare belief in fairies, magic, ghosts.

The clients of this café pick up papers and take seats,
backs turned to windows, where whatever outside happens
has the same charm as the news that testifies that nothing's changed.
They've tried on history's tragic mask so long
the next page is a replica of every one before.

Everything that's in me lies in each of these staid faces.
I have turned my whole attention to erasing the ennui
of day-long travel, in cramped armchairs in the sky,
from other rendezvous
where the familiar future pushes days along, each one
a template for the next, to come to this that feels like home.

Here, there: the present's stacked up like denial on denial,
and the avenue named Freedom's built on water,
but explore yourself, this place says: there's no radio
or music to abduct you, only streets that fill with thinkers
just like you in time-lapse study of each moment
and no camera but your eyes and ears,

such motion and such life, on this first morning, and the thought
of others like it and the foretaste of the cup, and why not,
do the same tomorrow when the dawn breaks here again.

The Good Life And Others

Poem: That Look Like Fun

FUN AT THE EXAMINERS' MEETING
The pass-rate's ninety-nine per cent again.
Now who believes we don't have standards?

SHOCKJOCK FUN
If a total stranger talking filth and bigotry
Invaded houses up and down the street
We'd call the ambulance or police.

BON APPETIT FUN
Everything we eat recalls
How well we've outsourced death.

REPETITIVE SHOCKJOCK FUN
He speaks like a parrot talking
In a language no one speaks.

The Cycle Path: A Walk In The Throwaway World

ducks once skimmed the surface,
dwelt in reeds here
where the garbage chokes the creek

bike chained to a street sign
all through March is gone this morning
but the cobwebs still remain

the magpie lands to watch
an Air Tractor swooping low
to spray the fields

first the dead bird turned to paste
then after one week's traffic,
silhouette

autumn and three students
up and trembling in the dew

the white of frosted elm
is not the white of frosted paths

nothing in bloom
but the Caltex sign
lone star in mist

young neighbours' loaded condoms,
empty beer cans on my lawn

pale blue of the watered-ouzo sky
and the white full moon low in the west

subtly then each small bud bursts
its bounds: the wattle's back

a week ago in the neat suburban yard I pass
the owner's head lay separate
from the body

the Chancellor's jet becomes a speck,
so he too, in my mind

dwarf cactus, plaster frogs and gnomes:
what country is this, friends?

the idiot boys stamp, whoop and sing
their fluting calls announcing spring

wind, if you had no avenues of poplars,
would you sigh?

track pants by the track again:
though it's zero, spring is here

nothing could defeat the pie;
not even the ibis touch it
where it stays on the freeway bridge

people with faces like potatoes
I meet on my morning walk

the growl of the diesel changing gears,
the all-day surf
of tyres on tar

Aplomb

We knew he had it in him,
steady purpose and ambition,

when he stood and drank all night,
a foaming schooner for each year he'd been alive,
no pause for eating. Time was short.

Somewhere in the room a wowser wailed
as cigarette smoke kippered barrackers' applause.

The hero on the amber ocean heard the sirens chanting
on the juke box, swallowed froth and tacked and yawed
into the night.

Station agents, watching, would recount it to their kids,
and lawyers boast of student days.

Women, sinking surreptitious Vera Lynns in kitchens,
and their spouses nipping rum in horsey bars
would now and then pause in their mission,
to compute the chance of bettering the score.

Rebel bikers visiting the town would prop their hogs
and call in silence, as if entering a shrine.

Field Study

Over all, the Lookout looms: town centre, pool,
Courthouse and schools. In Council, his chained Honour's
mind's fixated on the swine who dobbed him in
        to the Commission:

aldermen and solo alderwoman watch
his fingers serpenting desk furniture, mouth
framing words, mind feeling up that junior,
        yes, why not, tonight.

What? Fellow speculator breaks in on him:
Plaza plan, Mall, sidewalk café, boutique outlets,
bars where svelte young things like her, or better, hmm…,
        play hard to get while

CC television cameras pause and frame
each lovely flâneur's face, self-conscious grace,
just-perfect cocktail sipped as lawyers chat up
        smooth trade, jiggle keys,

backslap and bray, chance lines to checkout chicks,
'You'll never know unless you try it, nothing
ventured, no harm asking, love, just don't regret
        you knocked the offer'.

Rev-heads argue starting places meanwhile on
the Lookout where the dropkicks, late dog-walkers,
perves and cruisers eye each other, half a
        chance. It's Happy Hour.

Private Views

1

Stripping off her shirt beside the river
while the passers-by were drooping
in a heat-wave: that sweet girl
who made my young friend run
for cover back to Sydney:
such things happen in this world.

2

In this photograph, he seems
a brute who does what your face
with that look that feigns desire,
and your body shaped for pleasure
have invited; that sweet face
so fine, symmetrical, designed
to break the hearts of those who
see and know that they could never
be with you, but know that like
this picture you and he and they will fade.

3

I watched you while you threw yourself
at trash. He wasn't worth you.
But you raised him to a god.

My Swedish Life

From Pittsburg.
Packed with pride by Maria Ramo.
Thanks, Maria.

Gary Olen says the musty smell can be eliminated
by dry cleaning or by washing.
I have washed a dozen pre-worn Swedish Army shirts.

The price per unit was so small I ordered three,
and then found every unit has four shirts.
I'll be seeing my time out in Swedish Army shirts.

One thing concerning flaws, says Gary Olen,
each piece of my military equipment
may be up to fifty years old,

dyes may vary, and it's common to find fabric
flaws like stains, spots and discoloration.
These are military trademarks.

Gary Olen tells me I am wearing
one rare limited quantity surplus treasure
representing training, the adventure, the elite and those

who put their lives upon the line for country
and a cause that they believe in.
Every piece is truly one of a kind.

The placement of the types of emblems
differs from those pictured in the catalog.
I differ every time I wear a Swedish Army shirt.

I won't see a SAAB JAS 39 fly over Kabul or
a no-fly zone in Libya or be one of the fifty thousand Swedish men and women
on fulltime or part-time duty dressed in Swedish Army shirts.

But I will sport a Swedish Army shirt with flaws and stains
when I am eating köttbullar, or sweeping porches, or re-reading
Tomas Tranströmer in winter when the sky is full of rain.

Tales Out of School

1. He Says, She Says

'I'd like to know', says the girl who intends
to be married in autumn, 'if heaven is true

and it's made up of people like us'.
And she got married too. And the boy sitting next to her

says, 'I don't reckon there's any such place. If there is,
it's geometry, shapes', while he eyeballs her friend.

'You won't get in, anyway', says the friend,
who'll be smashed before midnight tonight;

'You'll be standing outside'. 'What do you mean?'
says the boy, who will soon be on night shift and noting

the names of the town's aristocracy asking for Room Number Six.
'I saw the way you were looking at me', says the girl

with the big night ahead. 'I've heard that boys who strip girls
with their eyes will never see heaven again'.

2. A Gift For Teaching

The Guru, Mister Whatsup, Oblomov, The Sleeping Beaut,
and Madame Lash and the Vampire Bat

are ensconced in the Common Room
when Mrs Ick Deen harrumphs in with the Pickled Dill

and the Human Egg for the Weekly Discipline meeting
that will gouge out ninety minutes of each life-

form locked in here with the Banshee Queen,
but no one's counting anything but the slabs of cake

that the Sleeping Beaut can put away
before lunch. The business is the Excellence

in Teaching gong: who'll get the colour-photocopied
sheet with the space (add name) and the Old Firm's logo.

But each one is convinced that no one else here has
what German language aptly calls the Gift.

Introduction to Composition 100

Hello, I come from Mars.
I speak a language that is used among the Dead.
Years before your birth, I knew exactly what you'd say.

Do not imagine that I cannot read your thoughts.
I've read much better, rarely worse.

Believe me, I am old enough to be
your fathers' father, and, for all you know, I am.

You understand, of course,
that your enrolment will result in death this year
for every one of your grandparents, but myself.

By this semester's end you should be able
to have spelt my name correctly at least once
in all the emails that you send to beg for mercy.

And in answer to your question, 'What will I do if I fail?'
and your assertion that your parents will destroy you
if you do, I recommend you make your Will before we start.

I grow nostalgic... at your age I watched the Lions
and the Christians at weekends. Such jolly times.

Cudgels and sharp blows were all we had of teachers' aids.

The Visiting Preacher Spills
The Good Oil On Acne At The Retreat

Acne is the surest sign of teenage self-pollution.
It begins with doubtful films and long phone calls,
the source of images and rays that weaken minds
and create habits that will cause the loss of sight.

Among teenagers, pressure to conform can mark
a generation lost to healthy thoughts:
androgynous pop 'idols', toilet language
and insistent modern music spread defilement.

Only books and papers without pictures
should be kept inside the house,
and children's clothes should be examined when
they've been out with their friends.

Bathrooms are the sites of unclean habits:
those who spend more time in there than the body's
health requires should be counselled by fit persons
trained in hygiene and attested by their pastors.

Guilty looks and whispering, as parents know,
are symptoms that a child is lost to vice.
Children who insist on keeping doors locked
and refuse to come when called may be the slaves of self-abuse.

Children who deny what they are thinking
when accosted should wear boxing gloves to bed.
In chronic cases, doors should be removed.
Acne is a sign of sordid minds.

And So Good Night

Curious to the end, Lavoisier
ordered a friend to make sure to look close at his eyes
when the blade had just severed his head.

He told him he'd blink if he had any consciousness left.
Doctor Guillotine's engine was quick,
and the head fell at once to the deck:

nothing there for the friend.
But it seems that the story's a myth,
circulated long after the death of the man who discovered

that air is a mix of the gases he named.
No, politics got him at length – that and shock
and the lack of O_2.

The last thing he did with his eyes
was to stare at the basket, not blink: blinking
calls things into play that a corpse doesn't have:

muscles working as well as the brain.
Who's surprised that he stared? John the Baptist,
in similar straits, was just meat on a plate:

Like Lavoisier, he'd said enough to get into that state
and who can say what he'd have blinked?
Nothing we read says he turned to Salome, and winked.

Defriend Me Here

I like the way that William Shawm remarks, as if
in passing, how his country stamps
on unobtrusive people. And there are so many of them.
But I pause. I know the problem.

While I'm searching in the Reject Shop and Trader Lou's
for screws and nails, a voice on amped-up radio's haranguing
me and all other mes who move, enchanted around the counters,
that a plague is on our houses.

I concur. The plague is threatening my health
as sure as eggs is avian ovarian by-products.
I would say its work is done. It is the voice,
that's soft and oily and then louder, till it snaps.

My fellow shoppers fondle produce
from Sri Lanka, Thailand, China, Bangladesh:
Used-by soups and pepper, shirts at crazy prices
with dead rock stars, manga popsies and tattoo-style monsters on them.

And the voice opines that desperate occasions call for—
here, the store that's crammed with mes vibrates
with passion in agreement or revulsion—urgent measures,
and the nerve to see it through.

We are at war, just like our fathers, our grandfathers
and those mothers gone before. Good workers those.
Yes I believe my life is threatened,
Here, transfixed in the cheap tools, I am giddy.

After all, we're men and women who know torture,
mutilation, death and rape are not so hot
unless it happens on the screen, and then who knows
what's real, what's not. I must be dreaming once again.

This shop's a tardis in no country that I know.
The language jetsam laps around me and the other mes
who fossick in the flotsam on the counters.
Hypnotised, we check our change and seek the street.

The Pursuit of Happiness

'To be stupid, selfish and have good health
are three requirements for happiness,
though if stupidity is lacking all is lost.'

— Gustave Flaubert

Happiness, your lower forms
keep oafs employed full-time
in proving misanthropes correct.
So all are pleased.

Americans adore your long strip tease,
the mad pursuit.
Sprung from a slaver's mind to a scrap of paper,
you still dance just out of reach.

Unhappiness of others lifts our spirits;
their despair's another matter.
Our composure goes to hell when they reveal
they have the nerve to try our patience.

Happiness may be locating someone
who agrees with us that language,
that attempts to prolong happiness,
will always make us laugh.

The Kabbala assures us
God's not happy but content
to grow more dark
while all creation can go figure.

Keats spoke for us all when he averred
he was a coward who could not endure
the pain of being happy.
Hold that thought.

Happiness will end as it begins
and we'll be wretched once again,
so why the effort? Misery and
disappointment never let us down.

The Good Life When It Happens

Postcards from museums make it seem that you exist,
but never here.

I thought I saw you going undercover years ago
The scent of lucerne, freshly mowed,
hung in the orchard where I walked to pilfer limes;

I heard the shadow of your cadence
in the lowing of the cows,
and in the tone of milk from teats into the pail;

I knew your texture in the organs
of the poultry that I gutted,
smelt you in the feathers plucked
and bodies rotting on the fence,
black snake and fox and feral moggy.

Falcons rode on thermals, scrutinising stubble fields;

Once, you made a raucous entrance
when a bull destroyed a fence
that kept him from the Jersey heifers.

Then you left, until I glimpsed you in your fancy dress
in books where you spoke Greek.
There, gods and men and women coupled
with each other and strange creatures in such fashions
as made schoolwork seem bizarre.

You changed address and blinked out now and then
in art and plays.
Shepherds sang in Tuscan
of their girlfriends' hair and snarls.

I hardly saw you while I hacked at gorse,
lantana, thistle, burr, to make a mulch,
nor until eels I trapped were smoked on hooks
I hung inside the chimney of my cabin.
Then you entered with the taste.

You go in mufti where a family waits at tables,
Trading gossip with regulars who sing at times,
conduct loud conversations, laugh and
stay so late that some remain all night.

Each morning on the pavement,
business-suited men and women drink their coffee,
standing straight beside high tables,
watching trams and buses pass.

They speak of deals and set their faces for the day
while older men inside play draughts, touch beads
and talk of football.

Intermittently, one stands and leaves
and shortly after passes by,
escorting some small grandchild off to school.

Prizes and certificates the patron won for shooting
line the walls.
His conversation runs along a stave when silence falls.

Strangers who call in to ask for cigarettes and matches
wonder what they're missing here.

Grafton Bridge

I'm living in a hotel once again.
The anchor on the flat screen reads the score.
No college in the USA is safe.
The shootists' record stands at 45.
It's autumn but it feels like winter here.
The weatherperson says it's three degrees.
The trees are bare. It's good to be alive.

I'm on the thirteenth floor of Waldorf,
looking at spaghetti roads below.
Six lanes siphon traffic into town.
Another six decant the overflow.
The road's a peristaltic pump of lights.
in Grafton Gully forty years ago,
I walked among the trees like any faun.

Can all these people work on Friday nights?
The cafes, gardens of cholesterol frights,
will all be packed. You haven't booked? Good luck.
The truth and beauty gang can't get enough.
The locals dine al fresco, to be seen.
The Depot's oca's roasted in duck fat.
A fan of Daffy's, I can't come at that.

Much has changed since Jeff Beck played Town Hall,
and more since Dr Tree played at the Globe.
A pity that the sirens sing so badly.
I've seen the buck's night clowns behaving madly
in the tranny bars along K Road.
Tables at the Beresford are crammed
beside the dosser with his lamb kebab.

Suspended in between the earth and sky,
my feet are planted on a concrete slab.
I like this building's chi-chi balconies
that ramp up dizziness and vertigo.
My neighbour says the feeling's like seasickness. I don't know.
They don't call these the Shaky Isles for nix.
I didn't go to Christchurch just for kicks.

I wonder how the ants keep track of days.
I'm sorry to announce I'm in their way.
My childrens' childrens' world will be insane.
I don't suppose the trains will run on time.
I wonder if the water will be fine.
A float plane's heading for St Marys Bay.
A Eurocopter bears the good and glamorous away.

The night's a pup. It's almost Saturday.
Unruly Id and ego slip the chain.
Vlad Putin's poison visage fills the screen.
Who'd suffer long-term pain to wipe out pain?
Another channel, porn that's on its knees.
Asceticism versus love of pleasure?
Bugger those, I'll walk the Middle way.

This time of night, the world's a hologram.
I'd better put my face on and be me.
Traffic sounds like sighs at a funeral, on the motorway,
Hydrodynamic noise around a reef.
The balcony dissolves. I'm on a bridge.
I'm almost wrapped in cloud and hear through rain
the shouts of people calling name to name.

The front door fronts the city's old boneyard.
Some epitaphs and names and dates die hard.
One begs, Oh, for the touch of a vanished hand
And the sound of a voice that is still.
'Scratch me', says a tourist to her partner,

leaning on the low stone wall. 'Scratch where?'
The streets announce found poems to the air.

The Grafton Bridge's span's twelve storeys high.
I lived when younger on the other side,
Concerned with Angst and bullshit some call life.
I often thought to slip off. What a mess.
The bridge was metaphor, stand-in for 'I have touched the sky'.
No point in being hung up all the time.
One day I'll die.

Night-Thoughts Young wrote epitaphs and bones,
procrastination is the thief, all that:
a poet for all seasons, Blake's and mine.
We need a cheer-up poetry, perhaps.
But I can't see it. O too happy love,
O happy women, and O happy chaps.
If I wrote verse like that I'd be a prat.

In my trans-ocean crossings,
on both sides the mood is bleak.
It may be there will come a time past mine
when something like compassion's back in vogue.
I wouldn't bet. Our willing executioners shout down
the weak or put them out of sight and hope and mind.
What more can any poem do but speak?

My forbears weighed their chances,
had enough of misery, and knew
some people die in some cursed ships at sea.
Does evil or injustice ever fade from memory?
What more could they invest in if they tried?
Walking on the quay, I recollect the heft of waves,
and listen for the turning of the tide.

Listening to the Prime Minister

Meeting you instead of hearing him,
the world is frisson. You're the taste
of that first apple that I bit. Fruit, amylase,
and juice ran down my face. Forever fresh
like heroin. Earth's hello with each kiss.
Like childhood? How could childhood be compared
with what an infant never knew?

Meanwhile, the news. In Germany,
two men agree to feast, and one declares,
'I am your meat'. The other eats him.
In Brazil, a man, his wife and mistress advertise.
They'd like a nanny. Two apply, and end up empadas.
They're delicious. Neighbours rush to buy a few.
That's advertising, word of mouth.

When he's talking, that's him, too.
As for you and me, we go to bed.
Waking, we learn people in the cradle of ideas—
like making gardens and inventing apricots—
for love of God are cutting off each others' heads.
I wonder whether people now unborn will one day
wonder how we took this in our stride, and why we did.

Look, his mouth is hovering above a microphone—
two inert things, and one of them's unmanned.
My love, we're history. So is he. We are embedded
with the dead, and those around us busy dying.
He takes lives to prove a theory.
Logic from his mouth beheads us too,
along with what we once thought good, or beautiful and true.

You say you like what is crazy in me.
I say I like what is crazy in you.

We don't live in his subjunctive.
Savagery, he says, should make us stronger,
like the Aztecs and Peruvians
who made their children meet
to meet their God.

John on Patmos

(*Hartman Schedel, 1440-1514: Queensland Gallery*)

— I will strike her children dead. *Revelations 2:23*

Real estate is wound up here
where a path spills down to the sea.

No magnificos' villas encroach.
The fish are allowed to be free.

Head inclined like a quizzical heron's,
an eagle stands on guard near the writer's knee

while the writer sits, inkwell in hand
beside a Matisse palm tree.

Above, remote, a child on her lap,
a woman's enthroned on a cloud.

The writer sees no strangeness there;
his eyes and mind are bowed

toward the text upon his lap
where stranger things appear:

the world in flames and children
weeping as it disappears.

The Simplicity of It

Like a word in a dictionary of a language no one speaks;
Like the space a bad book fills that still remains a space;
Like a phrase that makes a lean-to shelter for disgrace;
Like a body wrapped up in a bag in a public park;

Like the band of cloud above bulk tankers seen at dawn;
Like the eyes of kittens when they first walk out alone;
Like a shrine in China that's a sutra cut in stone;
Like the Graces governing the fates of sprats and men;

Like a sainthood warranting a party that's prevailed;
Like a dog, designed for eating, rolling on the beach;
Like the time in Israel when each man did as he wished;
Like a faded photograph that blows across a field;

Like epicures engulfing canapés at a consular ball;
Like a bird that skims the water – touch and go to air;
Like a rock that lands beside a policeman in the Square;
Like a replayed movie of a family funeral;

Like magpies in an elm tree clubbing in to feed the young;
Like a blindworm stranded on a bush trail in full view;
Like an aphorism that impersonates what's true;
Like the price that's always paid for licence of the tongue;

Like a broken submarine on the ocean's floor a week;
Like the newlyweds' first kiss when all the guests are gone;
Like the face of a man with the face of a weather-beaten prawn;
Like the roasting corpse that spits and hisses at the cook;

Like the abolition of emotion in a glance;
Like a market strewn with broken bodies in the sun;
Like a woman after dark who walks a path alone;
Like a farmer scooping soil to taste how sweet it is.

Like the call that comes at night when everyone's in bed;
Like the heirlooms pilfered while the body's barely cold;
Like a child's lost innocence before it's four years old;
Like Winged Victory hovering, with missing arms and head

The Stranger in the Crowd

A man in the crowd of commuters
standing at the railway station
felt a light touch on his forearm.

'Please excuse me', said the traveller,
'I am Death. What time's the train due?'

'I don't have a watch, but it is late',
the man replied.
'And your good self?' asked Death.

City Circle

Peta, Marijka from the suburbs
    and their horses, where are they?
        and concrete highways over Marijka's house,
            where is she now?

Men stand, beneath your window,
    urinating on the ferns, Adele.
        Where's Jane, tall as cornstalks?
            Silence welcomes her, with her gold hair.

Bobby wearing nights out with her lovers
    in a narrow bed, where is she?
        Grey Lynne, my brother's love
            below the sickle moon, where has she gone?

Gayle gone, my alter ego, lost
    inside the suburbs, where is she?
        Love shuffles round the kitchen floors
            no more for Virna, and for Katey in the dark.

Fast trains, bearing me to Libby
    and Katrina, Ruby, Pearl:
        will no one stay?
            Why must the lovely girls dissolve?

Sweet Lyn, someone's disappointment
    on the farm, has come to this:
        men stand, beneath her window, waiting
            till the dawn is pale across the Tasman.

Moons fade, and chimney pots of Newtown gleam
    again, and where in Petersham is Dany?
        Where is Wendy in the mountains?
            Bright blood blossoms as I hold Virginia's hand.

Calm peace wraps them up;
    as if they never slept,
        the streets are restless,
            and the graceful neon burns.

Punchbowl, where is Nancy, gone
    with all her artifice? The underground's
        dull roar caresses windows
            where she slept.

Slow couples, turning into air:
    the dust falls on them, on us.
        Men stand, beneath flats at the Junction,
            Double Bay, at Mosman, ceaseless.

Strange flowers, all their eyes are closed now
    that were eloquent where trains leave
        by the parks above the water where the bridge hangs
            still, enamoured of itself.

Boats leave, the McElhone Stairs empty,
    and dawn breaks, across the old jam factory, suburbs.
        Neon cools.
            An ice-man works the avenues of Potts Point

under Vivienne's tall terrace, where Helena watches
    liners leave, stairs empty, leaving them inside,
        enamoured, over traffic,
            on the balcony, caressed by eucalyptus.

Honeymooners walk below them, bashful
    on the pavements soused with rain;
        cats cry, taxis move about us.
            Nancy sleeps along a wall.

Trains leave, and cavalcades of faces
    pass below ground in the darkness
        throbbing dully in the bedrock
            and the black earth under ancient streets of Sydney.

Impromptu

The night I stayed with friends,
I saw the grandchild,
thirteen, was she now—
so shaken, on discovering
she had turned into a woman,
that speech left her:
not from shyness
in our presence but
bewildered at the world
that had unmade her.

When we'd eaten dinner
and dispersed to other rooms,
she reappeared along
the corridor, and sat down
at the piano and played
not once, but three times,
that same piece until
the house rang and
that instrument,
as if its heart was breaking,
beat with her.

A Bird At Evening

That bird outside knows something
with its evening cry, first long and short,

the following notes falling, trilling long,
the day's goodbye: what others, feeling melancholy,

might call mournful. I say, summing up the day's
work, jotting on the diary of the air.

Today I found two carcasses of birds along the path,
One old, the other very young. The common warbler.

What the bird's song says is here is something
to fill nothing, that cannot stay empty long.

Poems say this also. What the bird and I collect
is each day's emptiness. We give it back,

when things fall silent, start again, as if the
failure of each day is all we know, is all our art.

My Parents Don't Exist

A riff on Merwin

Why make a meal of it? My parents don't exist.
My father being dead two years, my mother
Newly tucked inside a box in clay beside him,
I drove westward with my brother who is living
To the house they'd made their home for forty years.
The old place echoed, as it should.

We reefed the curtains. Dust motes eddied on the table.
We were walking through a warehouse. Or an op shop.
Hungry ghosts, our sisters, had been there.
The beds were stripped, the sideboard gutted.
Dresses none of them would be seen wearing were mere cerements wrapping air.
A banshee neighbour came too late. There'd be no drinkies.

Every room a stage set, flats deserted by the actors:
Kitchen scentless, walls of air we called a parlour,
Ceiling pushing back the sky. Façade of silence.
Bathroom chrome museum where we'd seen our father shave,
Our sisters wash. The image-maker on the wall.
Time was, a toilet clogged with tampons.

Moving on, a vase that even burglars left as trash,
And painted plates my mother brought back from a town abroad we'd never seen,
The shelves of faces stored in albums no one wanted,
and a diary that my father willed I'd find, inside the false floor of a cupboard.
We took everything of use to others to the Salvos
and returned to find a sister had been there and gathered all that took her eye.

No use hexing her for heist of the coffee pot we'd brought.
My brother laughed. The herbs and shrubs around the garden
Were now memories like the roses and our mother's fondness for them.
No one we had known had lived in that house when we left.
We went our ways. My plane ascended, and I knew that I was free.

Returns of the Day

Dreams are unstinting: the dead come to life there,
touchable, brilliant. Their teeth are so white,
mouths so moist; their lips part as they welcome us.
                Why are they silent then?

Playing such sports as are lovely to watch,
Poised in the act of surrendering to sex,
those who walked next to us, smiling at what we said.
                Why not a word from them?

First loves and siblings and cousins and parents,
uncles who chaffed and cajoled, aunts who chivvied
us, coddled us: voices that barracked us,
                dumb, bid us come to them.

Nudge Nudge

Any nuance, any gesture gets me back to this,
Back to the human, back to thinking how it
Comes about I'm here and why, et cetera:
Does it matter? Destined to be dusted into urns, we evoke
Ennui in others. Evening creeps on pads of silent feet on city roofs.
Fat ugly autos prowl the suburb, driven by fat ugly folk.
Get out? Graffiti says 'Why look up here? You are the joke,
Hell isn't others, it's yourself'.
In 2010 all poets were aged thirty, even all of those long dead.
Just joshing. That's my business: I go fishing for bright words,
Kick sounds and ideas round, score goals, get into touch.
Life is after all no graceful sentence but a word.
Most spell it out. A micro-story.
No amount of saying yes negates the fact that no is underrated.
Over time, the mouth that is the origin of trouble
Proves that statues have the best time. No use
Querying their accent. They have earned their right to silence.
Reach no further for the why and how, etcetera,
See life steady see it whole, the gemlike flame that burns us up.
To burn, to live: we tidy up our mums and dads,
Usurp their thrones, their little plots, a little while. The children smile,
Veins full of juice, skin taut: they pole vault over us
While counting: vault or wall-niche, what's the cost?
Xylem feels like that when phloem tips the wink in passing:
You-tube action, up they go, while we go down to sink cells,
Zip from zenith. O the circulatory zing.

My Life as a Cowboy

Aurochs are not ibex
But they sound so close to oryx
Cataloguers can be flummoxed.
Don't be hoodwinked. It's not onyx.
Everywhere you find it, it's a black rock. So is ebony.
Flow gently traffic in the gully till I end my song.
Great pits of fashion have I known in modern life. Some
Highlights also. Say, reverse initial letters. That's me, guys.
In any case, it's iffy. It's a wonder Weil's disease bypassed our farm and
Jumped our neighbour's kiddies. As my father's cousin said, I reckon you can
Kiss your feet goodbye if you like standing in the cowpats on cold mornings.
Last time they'll write home to brag of life in the bucolics, saying boo-sucks.
Mostly we don't muck round with manure. Nor do old friends in Aystetten.
No fun taking chances with the picturesque conditions you can contract
On a farm. Hansi gave up wading in the Mist heap when he had to
Pump it out. Pure gold for maize. Ringworm, anybody? Anthrax?
Queen of spades each time, straight off the bottom of the deck.
Robert Frost was not a cowboy. Neither was Les Murray. Cows
Stand in Gruner's light at Bellingen and Bowral looking
Tired of holding poses. Boring. But when Martin asked
Us to Te Awamutu where he ran the butter factory,
Vowing never to go back to lighthouse keeping
When he married Ally, who said watching
Xemes and boobies wasn't her idea of
Yearlong fun, we said, considering
Zoo or zoetrope, no contest.

Wotif

My history is a fiction. This is footnote such and such.
I met as many writers who are dead
as those I know who now draw breath.
Anomaly: earth's population's more
than all of those who died and went before.
I thought of that at Millers where I bought
another bag of coffee from Brazil.

There's nothing leaving Auckland everyday.
Container vessels bring Japan onshore.
I think that I shall never see such Jeeps
with such low mileage on another city's streets.
There's seeming and some savour in Dom Road,
that takes me to the small Iranian shop
where that young midwife recommends fresh dates.

Lambrettas are the deuce for stable rides.
The Honda was less sexy. Still, I struck
a certain air of nonchalance. A cinch.
A Mod at heart, I thought myself unique,
but take no further questions here today.
Jim Baxter was renowned for speaking plain
but chuntered like a race tout. But he wrote,

and that made all the difference. He posed
as hero of a legend of himself.
It isn't easy being someone else,
and I remain a bit part in my script.
How many famous poets have I met?
Tuwhare, Hunt and Glover trading lines,
a comic trio in a sozzled heap.

The city's not what I found here when young
and I am not the me that I was then. Good grief,
is that the time? It's 3 a.m. Two cruise ships
from the Holland Line have docked. The language
on the street below depends. I keep a balanced diet,
eat Malay, Korean, Taiwanese and Thai.
The curry house proprietors know me.

My children speak in accents not my own,
grandchildren even less. They're on their own.
Auckland is a city I have dreamed.
Albert Park hosts beggars sleeping rough.
If no man is an island, some are reefs
society can break on. Public grief
sits easy with erasure of belief.

It's dog eat dog from street to shining street.
Our superstitions speak of common fates.
Walk under ladders? Mount the scaffold then.
A broken mirror? Throw it in the pond.
It holds your shattered image and your soul.
In India, opals signify good luck.
In England, like deaf white cats, they bring ill.

The people's clothes are made in Bangladesh.
Breathe deep and you can smell the burning flesh.
Garlic's planted when the moon declines.
What's mourning for except for settling spooks?
Far better to cut arms and legs and heads
from those who die, so we sleep safe in bed,
like Monika in *Nekromantic 2*.

The hotel where I sleep's *The Promised Land*.
I used to stay with friends, but who can stand
the morning chatter and the midnight bores?
Does anyone enjoy the third degree?
Hypocrisy begins at home. I'm free
to turn all night in fresher sheets or write
while drinking Ardbeg in the neon light.

CNN would like me to believe
the world is sound bites, Christiane Amanpour,
and market news through seven twenty-four.
They might as well chant paeans to Saint Jude.
The rain outside's a sieve of harbour views.
The sky's a dream of backdrop
to the maxims in the *Book of Disquietude*.

Willie Yeats called *Lear* and *Hamlet* gay.
Black Minnaloushe observed the moon
and smiled. The old boy's wits had gone astray.
Yeats preferred an ancient virelay
to lyrics his contemporaries made.
Listening to Lustmord every night.
The cat grew fat as Whitman, lucky wight.

The city that I knew has changed its stripes.
I wouldn't grieve for what it might have been.
The graves above the motorway decay
and buck me up. They're grief's Antipodes.
The trees are full of birdsong. After years
like water, I meet friends in supermarts,
discussing leeks and fennel soup and art.

Catullan Farewell

Now summer banishes cold nights
and gusty days.

Now skies of dripping clouds and southerlies
massage the crops and vines.

I leave behind high sclerophyll and pasturelands
for famous coastal cities.

Now my mind is fixed on moving
and my feet are getting toey.

Goodbye, friends and colleagues
who made what in life is pleasant,

you, who wandered here together and are leaving
for your homes by other roads.

To Silence

Thanks for being there
between the tinnitus and sirens
and the hiss of budded ears
of those around me on a train,
in airport lounges, in the Malls,

for interrupting sound at parties
when self-consciousness kicks in,
and could-be lovers check their banter,
take their thoughts to separate beds,
and when the mouth-rinse water's gone
with all that flowed since day began,

for being there when drunken laughter
of the neighbours wears itself out in the dark
of 4 a.m. or dawn
before the birds call greetings
or alarms around the globe.

You are the space between the petals
of the aural ikebana of the world,
the pause between the painter's brushstrokes,
and the proof sheet
and the poem that records
the dogged drumbeat of the heart.

Acknowledgments.

Versions of several of these poems have appeared in the *Australian*, *Blast*, *Communion*, *Cordite*, *Earthly Matters—Science Made Marvellous*, *Eureka Street*, *Island*, *Mascara*, *Perihelion*, *Prosopisia*, *Southerly*. One ('City Circle') appeared in the 1980 Fat Possum Press collection *Dawn Parade* (Armidale NSW), and three others in the 2017 Burringbar (Hobart) souvenir collection *In the Real World (and other poems)*.

www.ingramcontent.com/pod-product-compliance
Lightning Source LLC
Chambersburg PA
CBHW031001090426
42737CB00008B/632